THE GLORY STORY

John 20—21; Acts 1 FOR CHILDREN

Written by Walter Wangerin Jr.

Illustrated by Don Kueker

ARCH Books

COPYRIGHT © 1974 CONCORDIA PUBLISHING HOUSE, ST. LOUIS, MISSOURI

MANUFACTURED IN THE UNITED STATES OF AMERICA

ALL RIGHTS RESERVED

ISBN 0-570-06083-4

Publishing House
St. Louis

My name is Matthias—not much of a name;
I'm four feet ten inches, a little bit lame,
A little bit chubby, a little bit bald,
And blowing my nose all the time with a cold.
Not much of a name, not much of a size,
Not much of a *man* in other men's eyes.

I had to climb trees to see anything neat,
While other men stood on their feet in the street.
I was mad at my brothers, all taller than I;
I was mad at the sparrows because they could fly;

I was mad at the horses because they could run;
I was mad at the moon and upset with the sun,
And I generally didn't like anyone.

But I changed! I changed! I changed for the better,
Like thunder clouds changing to summer-sky weather.
Mary and Thomas and Peter came by
To tell me that Jesus the Lord was alive!
I had to be glad after that, don't you see?
Well, here is the way that it happened to me.

Many Easters ago when the evening was smoggy
And murky and muggy and filthy and foggy,
I was walking and coughing and blowing my nose
And sneezing and slipping and stubbing my toes—
Till I fell on my face in the mud; and I cried.

I didn't get up. Why *should* I have tried?
Those were the days when my Jesus had died,
And I didn't care; I just didn't care.
But suddenly Mary was at my side,
Pinching my ear and pulling my hair,
And grinning as wide as a whole piece of pie.
"Matthias!" she said, "Matthias, don't hide.
I saw Jesus around and about and alive!"

Then she told me a story that I couldn't miss:
"Matthias," she said, "I was standing beside
His empty grave and making two fists,
When a man came by. Well, I jumped up and cried,
'Hey Mister! Hey you! What did you do?
Where did you steal my Jesus to?'

"But that Man said my name: 'Mary,' He said.
Matthias, our Jesus—He isn't dead,
He's alive; He's the one who said 'Mary' to me!
Matthias, get up and come running to see."
Then Mary left, dancing and singing with glee.

Well, Mary was happy, but what about me?
I hadn't seen Jesus the Lord, don't you see,
Or touched His right hand
or His shoulder — who knows?
It might've been someone else wearing His clothes!

I didn't get up; I just didn't care.
No one had proved it to *me* He was there.
But then another man happened by,
Thomas, grinning like *two* pieces of pie.

"Matthias," he said, "Matthias, you ape,
Our Jesus just walked through a purple drape,
And here you lie like a sack on your back!
Listen," he said, "and I'll tell you a lot.
The doors on our bedroom were all firmly locked;

We were hiding inside, ashamed and afraid
That the soldiers would round us all up in a raid.
John said that Jesus had been there before,
But I said, 'You liar,' for I wanted more:
I wanted to *touch* Him; and then, I was sore
That they had forgotten about me before.

"But Matthias, Matthias, Matthias, guess what?
The windows were shuttered as tight as a nut,
But Jesus walked straight
through that drape all the same.
'Thomas,' He said; He called me by name.
Oh, I crawled in the corner for shame.
'Touch me,' He said, 'and see, I'm the same
Who went to the cross for you, Thomas, and died.'
Matthias, Matthias, I wanted to hide;
But I touched His hands, His feet, and His side;
And He was the Christ—our Lord and our God!

"Matthias, you ape, get up off the sod,
Dance, laugh, cheer!
Make it perfectly clear
To all that you meet,
That the Lord's on His feet!"
And Thomas went dancing on down the road,
Laughing and skipping and crying aloud: "ALIVE!"

Now, what they were saying was getting to me,
And I was as hungry as I could be.
But before I could rise to get something to eat,
Peter came by in his stocking feet.

"Matthias, He cooked us our breakfast," he said,
"Some fish and some wine, a small slice of bread,
Enough to last us forever, He said.
And He told me to tell you this glorious news.
(Why, I didn't have time to put on my shoes.)
He lives!" And Peter went dancing away.

Then seventy people came running to say,
"Matthias, Matthias, get up right away:
Jesus is coming to see us today!"
And I did! I did! I stood on my toes!
I laughed! I danced, went running with those
Who know what every last Christian knows:
That Jesus the Christ is alive.
Bless me, I grinned like *five* pieces of pie.

Then we saw Jesus, as real as you please,
Telling the lot of us, down on our knees,
To baptize, to preach to each person we found.
Then he rose to his toes and left the ground,
Above our eyes, above the skies,
Above the morning and the sound
Of people grinning on the ground,
Grinning like seventy pies.

I am short, I am chubby, I don't have much hair,
But these things don't matter, and I couldn't care:
I was changed to a special man back there.
I was made a disciple with Peter and Thomas
To preach that the Lord is alive and among us.

DEAR PARENTS:

At the beginning of *The Glory Story,* Matthias felt like most of us do now and then. He was completely down and out. If left to himself, he might have stayed in the mud of his despair and self-hate forever. But he wasn't left to himself. He was lifted up by a strength greater than any mortal man's, the strength of the risen Lord.

But how did this strength reach him and grab hold? Not through a flash of lightning or a thunderous voice. Christ reached out through the hands of simple people, people who were so filled with the wonder of His Good News that they just had to share it with someone less fortunate. Matthias' character is fictionally expanded, but his story is as true as the love of our Lord. It happens every day and will go on happening as long as there are souls that need to be lifted up from their sins and despair.

Ask your child why Matthias felt bad. What happened to make him feel better? How did he find out what Jesus had done? Can you think of any people today who are sad like Matthias was? How do you suppose you could help them feel better?

How about teaching your child this ancient Easter greeting: "Christ is risen." "He is risen indeed!"

THE EDITOR